SUPERWOMEN
ROLE MODELS

MELINDA GATES

Christine Honders

PowerKiDS
press™

New York

Published in 2017 by The Rosen Publishing Group, Inc.
29 East 21st Street, New York, NY 10010

First Edition

Editor: Katie Kawa
Book Design: Reann Nye

Photo Credits: Cover, pp. 1–32 (halftone pattern) Solomin Andrey/Shutterstock.com; cover, p. 1 Larry Busacca/Getty Images Entertainment/Getty Images; pp. 5, 24 ALAIN GROSCLAUDE/AFP/Getty Images; p. 7 Monica Schipper/FilmMagic/Getty Images; p. 9 Brian Ach/Getty Images Entertainment/Getty Images; pp. 11, 25 ERIC FEFERBERG/AFP/Getty Images; p. 13 Oli Scarff/Getty Images News/Getty Images; p. 15 lembi/Shutterstock.com; p. 17 The India Today Group/Getty Images; p. 19 THEMBA HADEBE/AP Images; p. 21 DON EMMERT/AFP/Getty Images; p. 23 FRANCOIS GUILLOT/AFP/Getty Images; p. 27 Justin Sullivan/Getty Images News/Getty Images; p. 29 Bryan Bedder/Getty Images Entertainment/Getty Images; p. 30 Chesnot/Getty Images News/Getty Images.

Library of Congress Cataloging-in-Publication Data

Honders, Christine, author.
 Melinda Gates / Christine Honders.
     pages cm. — (Superwomen role models)
 Includes index.
 ISBN 978-1-5081-4832-6 (pbk.)
 ISBN 978-1-5081-4776-3 (6 pack)
 ISBN 978-1-5081-4809-8 (library binding)
 1. Gates, Melinda, 1964—Juvenile literature. 2. Bill & Melinda Gates Foundation—History—Juvenile literature. 3. Women philanthropists—United States—Biography—Juvenile literature. 4. Humanitarianism—United States—Juvenile literature. I. Title.
 HV28.G326H66 2017
 361.7'632092—dc23
 [B]
                                   2015032212

Manufactured in the United States of America

CPSIA Compliance Information: Batch #BS16PK: For Further Information contact Rosen Publishing, New York, New York at 1-800-237-9932

CONTENTS

A LIFE OF GIVING

Role models are seen by others as people to be imitated. They live in ways that make us want to be like them. Melinda Gates is often called a role model. She's the **co-chairperson** of the largest charitable foundation in the world. It's called the Bill & Melinda Gates Foundation, which is named after her and her husband, Bill Gates.

Melinda has dedicated her life to improving the education and health of people all over the world. She's especially concerned with improving these areas for women and children. Melinda believes giving women more opportunities and access to better health care will change the world for the better. She's doing her part to help make that happen. Melinda is a role model for all people because of her belief in giving her time, energy, and money to help those who need it.

IN HER WORDS

"Empowered women—women who are healthy, can exercise some decision-making power, and have some economic means—make life better for everybody in the community."
Interview with the *Daily Mail*, published on April 25, 2015

Melinda Gates has spent her life learning. When she was young, she enjoyed learning about math and computers. Now, she's learning about the best ways to help people around the world.

YOUNG LIFE

Melinda Gates was born Melinda Ann French in Dallas, Texas, on August 15, 1964. She has one older sister and two younger brothers. Her father, Ray French, was an engineer. Her mother, Elaine French, stayed at home to raise their children. Her family managed rental properties as a way to earn extra money. Melinda mowed lawns, cleaned the properties, and did anything else she could to help with the family business.

Melinda became interested in computers when she took an advanced math class in seventh grade. In 1982, she graduated as the **valedictorian** of the Ursuline Academy of Dallas, which is an all-girls high school. Education was important in Melinda's family, and it continues to be important to Melinda today.

Melinda's parents taught her the value of hard work. They also encouraged her love of math and computers at a time when girls didn't often focus on those subjects.

COLLEGE AND CAREER

Melinda went to college at Duke University in North Carolina. She graduated with bachelor's degrees in computer science and economics in 1986. She earned a master's degree in **business administration** one year later from Duke University's Fuqua School of Business. That same year, she moved to Seattle, Washington, to take a job as a project manager at Microsoft Corporation, which is one of the largest computer software companies in the world.

Melinda worked at Microsoft for nine years and eventually became a general manager of information products. Some of the projects she worked on included Expedia, which is a popular website that helps people plan trips, a movie guide called Cinemania, and an online encyclopedia called Encarta.

MELINDA AND BILL

Bill Gates is a computer programmer who's also one of the founders of Microsoft Corporation. He's one of the most famous computer pioneers in the world, and he's one of the wealthiest people alive today. By the time Melinda joined Microsoft in 1987, Bill was already a billionaire. After dating for a few years, he and Melinda were married in 1994. Their marriage is a partnership between people who both want to do whatever they can to help others.

Melinda and Bill Gates were married in Hawaii on January 1, 1994. They believe in working together to help make the world a better place.

STARTING A FAMILY

Melinda and Bill had their first child—a girl named Jennifer Katherine—in 1996. That year, Melinda decided she would leave Microsoft to raise her family and focus on charity work. After that decision was made, she and Bill had a son, Rory John, and another daughter, Phoebe Adele.

When their children were born, Bill and Melinda were already two of the wealthiest people in the world. However, that didn't mean their children wouldn't have to work hard. Both Melinda and Bill grew up in working families, and they wanted their children to understand the value of hard work. Their children had chores, were given allowances, and were taught the value of earning and saving money. Melinda made sure business never got in the way of their family life.

IN HER WORDS

"That's another reason why it's important for me to be a role model, particularly for my girls to see what it's like to be a woman and do that juggle between work life and family life."
Interview with Cable News Network (CNN), published on September 5, 2013

Melinda travels often because of her work. She sometimes plans these trips around her children's school breaks so they can all go together.

THE WILLIAM H. GATES FOUNDATION

In 1994, Melinda and Bill started their first charitable foundation with Bill's father, William H. Gates Sr. One reason the William H. Gates Foundation was created was to honor Bill's mother, Mary Maxwell Gates, who was a lifelong **philanthropist** who died earlier that year. Many of its first projects were focused on helping people in the Pacific Northwest region of the United States, which is where the Gates family lived. The foundation also addressed global educational and health issues.

Three years later, Melinda and Bill started the Gates Library Foundation, which focused on bringing computers and Internet access to public libraries across the United States. In 1999, its name was changed to the Gates Learning Foundation to highlight its goal of providing **minority** students with scholarship money so they could go to college.

Melinda and Bill both believe in the importance of public libraries, so supporting libraries has always been a part of their charitable efforts.

THE BILL & MELINDA GATES FOUNDATION

In 2000, Melinda, Bill, and Bill's father combined their foundations, and the Bill & Melinda Gates Foundation was born. That year, it had an **endowment** of $17 billion! Much of that money came from Melinda and Bill personally. They've been considered among the most generous philanthropists in the world for over 15 years.

The Bill & Melinda Gates Foundation continued its focus on education with the Gates Millennium Scholarship Program, which gave $1 billion to help increase educational opportunities for minorities. It also set aside $350 million to give to schools across the United States. Melinda worked hard to expand the foundation's vision toward global health issues and poverty, giving millions of dollars to organizations that make sure people living in poor countries are **vaccinated** against deadly diseases.

IN HER WORDS

"The premise of this foundation is one life on this planet is no more valuable than the next."
Interview with KOMO News in Seattle, Washington, published on November 4, 2004

The Bill & Melinda Gates Foundation gave $3.9 billion to charitable causes in 2014. Melinda plays a large part in deciding how that money is divided.

In 2006, billionaire investor and philanthropist Warren Buffet—who's also a friend of Melinda and Bill—announced a plan to give the Bill & Melinda Gates Foundation $30 billion. With this donation, it was expected that the foundation would grow to be worth nearly $60 billion in 20 years. That made the Bill & Melinda Gates Foundation the world's largest private charitable foundation.

At that point, the Bill & Melinda Gates Foundation was reorganized. Today, the foundation has four parts, each focusing on something Melinda and Bill strongly believe in: global health, global development, global policy, and education and community issues in the United States.

THE ORACLE OF OMAHA

Warren Buffet is a businessman who started running his first businesses when he was 13. After graduating from college in 1956, he became a successful investor in his hometown of Omaha, Nebraska. His investments made him extremely rich and earned him the nickname "The **Oracle** of Omaha." As of 2015, his total worth was estimated to be over $72 billion. The money he gave to the Bill & Melinda Gates Foundation in 2006 was over 80 percent of his fortune at that time.

Warren Buffett (right), Melinda Gates, and Bill Gates are all working to use their wealth to improve other people's quality of life.

Melinda had worked hard to keep her life private, especially when her children were young. However, with all her children in school in 2008, Melinda stepped into the public eye to begin her career as an **advocate** for those who are less fortunate.

GLOBAL HEALTH

Melinda's interest in global health issues was sparked after a trip to Africa in 1993. She and Bill traveled to the continent to go on an African safari. Traveling through poor villages, Melinda was shocked to see the conditions in which people were living. This trip started a journey of learning and philanthropy that still continues for Melinda and her husband.

Melinda came back a changed person. She learned that thousands of African children die each year from diseases such as **measles** and **malaria**. HIV, which is a deadly **virus**, is another huge problem in Africa. Of all the people infected with HIV around the world, over two-thirds of them live in Africa. Because many Africans are poor, they can't get the vaccinations and medications they desperately need to treat and prevent these diseases.

IN HER WORDS

"I would say that's true of the foundation today for Bill and me: It continues to be a learning journey." **Interview with *The Telegraph*, published on November 25, 2014**

Melinda and Bill have returned to Africa many times and donated millions of dollars to get medicines and vaccines to people who need them but can't afford them. In 2014, they announced they'd donate $50 million to help stop the spread of a deadly disease called Ebola that kills many people in Africa.

STANDING UP FOR WOMEN

Another thing Melinda noticed on her first trip to Africa was the unequal way women were treated. She saw women balancing huge bundles on their heads and carrying babies while walking barefoot through town. The men, however, walked around empty-handed, wearing shoes. Melinda started to ask herself questions about the needs of these women and how she could help.

Melinda made women's health issues one of the main focuses of the Global Health Division of the Bill & Melinda Gates Foundation. The foundation is dedicated to assisting women with family planning, as well as getting proper health care and nutrition to pregnant women and newborn babies. Another important issue for Melinda is equality for women and girls in parts of the world that aren't used to giving them the same rights as men.

Melinda has teamed up with other superwomen role models, such as Chelsea and Hillary Clinton, to speak out about equality for women around the world.

During her trips to Africa, Melinda would visit villages and speak to women personally. She learned that empowering women and girls could be a challenge. Not only are they very poor, but many of them are a part of societies where women have never been valued as highly as men. Some women wouldn't speak up for themselves. Melinda saw that giving women access to health care wasn't enough if they weren't confident enough in themselves to ask for it or to use it.

In 2014, Melinda wrote an article for *Science* magazine. She wrote that research shows when women are involved in family finances and in making health-care decisions, the health and well-being of their families improve. She also wrote that an important part of gender equality is education for both women and men.

Melinda believes all charitable organizations—including her own foundation—must do a better job of empowering women and putting women and girls at the center of the work they do.

INVESTING IN WOMEN

In her *Science* magazine article, Melinda declared that the Bill & Melinda Gates Foundation would do more to address the specific needs of women around the world. Melinda continues her fight in the United States, too. In an article she wrote for *Fortune* magazine in 2015, she encouraged people to hire more women, saying that the skills and vision they bring to the workplace is good for business. In that article, she wrote, "When you invest in women, you invest in the people who invest in everybody else."

DEVELOPMENT AROUND THE WORLD

Around 2.5 billion people around the world live on less than $2 a day. More than 1 billion people don't get enough food to eat.

The Global Development Division of the Bill & Melinda Gates Foundation works to get food, water, and shelter to poor people around the world. It teaches people about **sanitation** and the importance of keeping their water supply clean. This division works with local farmers and organizations that develop new varieties of crops through science to boost food production and fight hunger.

The Bill & Melinda Gates Foundation has a goal of preventing 1.8 million deaths related to **malnutrition** by 2020. Nutrition for all people—and especially for mothers and babies—is a cause close to Melinda's heart.

The Global Development Division also helps people out of poverty by giving them access to computers and the Internet, which increases their chance of getting an education. Access to the Internet also gives people more information about health care, especially for women and children.

EDUCATION AT HOME

Education in the United States is just as important to Melinda as education in other parts of the world. The Bill & Melinda Gates Foundation has given over $6 billion to the U.S. education system. The foundation is focused on fixing the inequalities in public school systems where schools in poor neighborhoods have lower test scores and higher dropout rates than schools in wealthier neighborhoods.

Melinda and Bill want to make sure students are prepared for college—no matter what their background is. Their foundation has supported new educational standards that are more closely related to what colleges and employers are looking for.

The foundation has supported efforts to get teachers more planning and training time. It's also given teachers access to technology that supports their work.

IN HER WORDS

"I know the difference a great teacher can make."
Interview with the Associated Press, given in November 2013

The Bill & Melinda Gates Foundation has given $1 billion to Washington State to be used toward education, as well as efforts to reduce poverty and homelessness.

A WOMAN TO BE IMITATED

Melinda Gates has been called one of the most powerful women in the world. Her work has inspired many people, and she's even inspired entire governments to help fund some of her most important projects.

In 2009, Melinda and Bill joined Warren Buffet to create a campaign called the Giving Pledge. By signing this pledge, Melinda and Bill promised to give at least half their wealth to charitable causes.

Melinda's life could have been very easy. Instead, she travels to the poorest countries in the world, dedicating her time to the people who live there. Her goal is to make their lives better. Melinda's a woman to be imitated. We can follow her example by doing what we can with what we have to help those in need.

GET INVOLVED!

How can you be more like Melinda? Volunteering in your community is a great place to start! There are organizations around the United States that need volunteers if you're interested in getting involved with some of the causes Melinda cares about. The Youth Volunteer Corps of America focuses on the individual needs of poor communities and inspires young people to work as a team to help meet those needs.

Melinda Gates is dedicated to helping people live full and healthy lives. Her dedication to others is what makes her a role model.

TIMELINE

August 15, 1964: Melinda Ann French is born in Dallas, Texas.

1982: Melinda graduates from the Ursuline Academy of Dallas and begins studying computer science and economics at Duke University.

1987: Melinda earns a master's degree in business administration from Duke University and begins working for Microsoft.

1993: Bill Gates and Melinda take their first trip to Africa.

1994: The William H. Gates Foundation is established.

January 1, 1994: Melinda and Bill are married.

1996: Melinda leaves Microsoft to focus on her family and her philanthropic work.

2000: The Bill & Melinda Gates Foundation is created.

June 2006: Warren Buffett donates nearly $30 billion to the Bill & Melinda Gates Foundation.

2009: Melinda and Bill sign the Giving Pledge.

2014: Melinda and Bill give $50 million toward the fight against Ebola.

2015: *Forbes* magazine names Melinda the third most powerful woman in the world.

GLOSSARY

advocate: A person who argues for or supports a cause.

business administration: A college program of study that teaches students how to run a business.

co-chairperson: A person who works with one or more people as the leader of an organization.

endowment: A large amount of money given to an organization to support it.

malaria: A serious disease with chills and a fever that is spread by the bite of a mosquito.

malnutrition: An unhealthy condition that results from not eating enough food or not eating enough healthy food.

measles: A disease that causes a fever and red spots on the skin.

minority: A group of people who are different from a larger group in a country or other area in some way, such as race or religion.

oracle: A person known for wise decisions or opinions.

philanthropist: A wealthy person who gives their money and time to help make life better for other people.

sanitation: The process of keeping places free from dirt and disease.

vaccinate: To give someone a shot to keep them safe from an illness.

valedictorian: The student with the highest grades in a graduating class.

virus: A very small living thing that causes disease and spreads from one person or animal to another.

INDEX

WEBSITES

Due to the changing nature of Internet links, PowerKids Press has developed an
online list of websites related to the subject of this book. This site is updated regularly.
Please use this link to access the list: www.powerkidslinks.com/sprwmn/melg